M000159668

The Very Best of
John Williams
INSTRUMENTAL SOLOS

Project Manager: Carol Cuellar
Cover Design: Martha Ramirez and Joseph Klucar
Arranged by Bill Galliford, Ethan Neuburg, and Tod Edmondson
Production Coordinator: Karl Bork

WARNER BROS. PUBLICATIONS
A Warner Music Group Company
USA: 15800 NW 48th Avenue, Miami, FL 33014

INTERNATIONAL MUSIC PUBLICATIONS LIMITED
ENGLAND: GRIFFIN HOUSE,
161 HAMMERSMITH ROAD, LONDON W6 8BS

© 2004 WARNER BROS. PUBLICATIONS
All Rights Reserved

Any duplication, adaptation or arrangement of the compositions contained in this collection requires the written consent of the Publisher.
No part of this book may be photocopied or reproduced in any way without permission. Unauthorized uses are an infringement of the U.S. Copyright Act and are punishable by law.

John Williams

John Williams was born in New York and moved to Los Angeles with his family in 1948. There he attended UCLA, Los Angeles City College, and studied composition privately with Mario Castelnuovo-Tedesco. After service in the Air Force, Mr. Williams returned to New York to attend Juilliard University, where he studied piano with Madame Rosina Lhevinne. While in New York, he also worked as a jazz pianist, both in clubs and on recordings. He then returned to Los Angeles, where he began his career in the film industry, working with such composers as Bernard Herrmann, Alfred Newman, and Franz Waxman. He went on to write music for many television programs in the 1960s, winning four Emmy Awards for his work.

Mr. Williams has composed the music and served as a music director for more than one hundred films, including *The Terminal, Harry Potter and the Prisoner of Azkaban, Harry Potter and the Chamber of Secrets, Minority Report, Star Wars*: Episode II *Attack of the Clones, Harry Potter and the Sorcerer's Stone, A.I. Artificial Intelligence, The Patriot, Angela's Ashes, Star Wars*: Episode I *The Phantom Menace, Stepmom, Saving Private Ryan, Amistad, Seven Years in Tibet, The Lost World, Rosewood, Sleepers, Nixon, Sabrina, Schindler's List, Jurassic Park, Home Alone, Home Alone 2, Far and Away, JFK, Hook, Presumed Innocent, Born on the Fourth of July*, the *Indiana Jones* trilogy, *The Accidental Tourist, Empire of the Sun, The Witches of Eastwick, E.T.* (the *Extra-Terrestrial), Superman, Close Encounters of the Third Kind*, the *Star Wars* trilogy, *Jaws*, and *Goodbye, Mr. Chips*. He has received forty-two Academy Award nominations, most recently for his score from Steven Spielberg's latest film *Catch Me If You Can*, making him the Academy's most nominated living person. He has been awarded five Oscars, three British Academy Awards, eighteen Grammys, three Golden Globes, four Emmys, and numerous gold and platinum records.

In January 1980, Mr. Williams was named nineteenth conductor of the Boston Pops Orchestra since its founding in 1885. He currently holds the title of Boston Pops laureate conductor, which he assumed following his retirement in December 1993 after fourteen highly successful seasons. Mr. Williams also holds the title of artist-in-residence at Tanglewood.

Mr. Williams has written many concert pieces, including two symphonies, a cello concerto premiered by Yo-Yo Ma and the Boston Symphony Orchestra at Tanglewood in 1994, concertos for the flute and violin recorded by the London Symphony Orchestra, concertos for the clarinet and tuba, and a trumpet concerto, which was premiered by the Cleveland Orchestra and their principal trumpet Michael Sachs in September 1996. His bassoon concerto, "The Five Sacred Trees," which was premiered by the New York Philharmonic and principal bassoon player Judith LeClair in 1995, was recorded by Mr. Williams with Ms. LeClair and the London Symphony Orchestra and has recently been released by Sony Classical to critical acclaim. In addition, Mr. Williams has composed the well-known NBC theme "The Mission," "Liberty Fanfare" composed for the rededication of the Statue of Liberty, "We're Lookin Good!" composed for the Special Olympics in celebration of the 1987 International Summer Games, and themes for the 1984, 1988, and 1996 Summer Olympic games and the 2002 Winter Olympic Games.

His concert work "Seven for Luck" for soprano and orchestra, a seven-piece song cycle based on the texts of former U.S. Poet Laureate Rita Dove, was given its world premiere by the Boston Symphony under Mr. Williams with soprano Cynthia Haymon at Tanglewood in 1998. Mr. Williams also composed his "American Journey," an orchestral work written to commemorate the new millennium and to accompany the retrospective film *The Unfinished Journey* directed by Steven Spielberg. The film and music were premiered at the "America's Millennium" concert in Washington, D.C., New Year's Eve 1999. Mr. Williams recently premiered a new concerto for French horn and orchestra, a work that was commissioned by the Chicago Symphony Orchestra for their principal horn, Dale Clevenger.

Many of Mr. Williams' film scores have been released as recordings; the soundtrack album *Star Wars* has sold more than four million copies, making it one of the most successful non-pop albums in recording history. Mr. Williams' highly acclaimed series of albums with the Boston Pops Orchestra began in 1980 on the Philips label, for which he recorded *Pops in Space; Pops on the March; Aisle Seat; Pops Out of This World; With a Song in My Heart* (a collaboration with soprano Jessye Norman); *America, the Dream Goes On* (a collection of favorite Americana); *Swing, Swing, Swing; Pops in Love; By Request...* (featuring music composed by John Williams); Holst's *The Planets; Salute to Hollywood*; and an all-Gershwin album entitled *Pops by George*. In 1990, John Williams and the Boston Pops started making recordings exclusively for the Sony Classical label. To date, these have included *Music of the Night* (an album of contemporary and classical show tunes); *I Love a Parade* (a collection of favorite marches); *The Spielberg/Williams Collaboration* (featuring John Williams' music for Steven Spielberg's films); *The Green Album* (which includes "This Land Is Your Land," "Simple Gifts," and "Theme for Earth Day"); a Christmas album entitled *Joy to the World*; an album of music by George Gershwin, Cole Porter, Richard Rodgers, and Jerome Kern entitled *Unforgettable*; a tribute to Frank Sinatra entitled *Night and Day*; an album featuring music by John Williams and Aaron Copland entitled *Music for Stage and Screen; It Don't Mean a Thing If It Ain't Got That Swing*, with vocalist Nancy Wilson; and *Williams on Williams: The Classic Spielberg Scores*. Mr. Williams' most recent recording with the Boston Pops Orchestra is entitled *Summon the Heroes*, the title track of which was the official theme for the 1996 Summer Olympics in Atlanta.

Mr. Williams has led the Boston Pops Esplanade Orchestra on United States tours in 1985, 1989, and 1992 and on a tour of Japan in 1987. He led the Boston Pops Orchestra on tours of Japan in 1990 and 1993. In addition to leading the Boston Symphony Orchestra at Symphony Hall and at Tanglewood, Mr. Williams has appeared as guest conductor with a number of major orchestras, including the London Symphony, the Cleveland Orchestra, the Philadelphia Orchestra, the Chicago Symphony, the Pittsburgh Symphony, the Dallas Symphony, the San Francisco Symphony, and the Los Angeles Philharmonic, with which he has appeared many times at the Hollywood Bowl. Mr. Williams holds honorary degrees from twenty American universities, including The Juilliard School, Berklee College of Music in Boston, Boston College, Northeastern University, Tufts University, Boston University, the New England Conservatory of Music, the University of Massachusetts at Boston, The Eastman School of Music, and the Oberlin Conservatory of Music. Mr. Williams also recently served as the grand marshal of the 2004 Rose Parade in Pasadena.

(June 2004)

Contents

CANTINA BAND

Music by
JOHN WILLIAMS

Moderately fast ragtime ($\jmath$ = 112)

Cantina Band - 4 - 1
IFM0427CD

© 1977 WARNER-TAMERLANE PUBLISHING CORP. (BMI) and BANTHA MUSIC (BMI)
All Rights Administered by WARNER-TAMERLANE PUBLISHING CORP.
All Rights Reserved

To Coda ⊕

Cantina Band - 4 - 2
IFM0427CD

DUEL OF THE FATES

Music by
JOHN WILLIAMS

Maestoso, with great force (♩ = 44)

Allegro (♩ = 152)

Duel of the Fates - 8 - 1
IFM0427CD

© 1999 BANTHA MUSIC (BMI)
All Rights Administered by WARNER-TAMERLANE PUBLISHING CORP.
All Rights Reserved

FAWKES THE PHOENIX

Music by
JOHN WILLIAMS

Moderato (♩. = 60)

Fawkes the Phoenix - 4 - 1
IFM0427CD

© 2002 WARNER-BARHAM MUSIC, LLC (BMI)
All Rights Administered by **WARNER-TAMERLANE PUBLISHING CORP.** (BMI)
All Rights Reserved

*An easier 8th-note alternative figure has been provided.

42

HARRY'S WONDROUS WORLD

Music by
JOHN WILLIAMS

Broadly (♩ = 160)

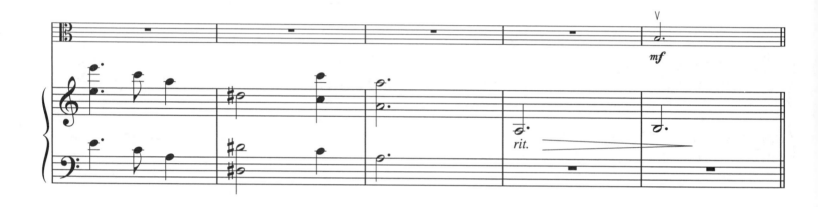

10 Stately and nobly (♩ = 120)

Harry's Wondrous World - 8 - 1
IFM0427CD

© 2001 WARNER-BARHAM MUSIC, LLC (BMI)
All Rights Administered by WARNER-TAMERLANE PUBLISHING CORP. (BMI)
All Rights Reserved

66

101 Stately and nobly

legato

*The top cue notes are provided as a performing alternative.

HEDWIG'S THEME

Music by
JOHN WILLIAMS

Misterioso (♩ = 160)

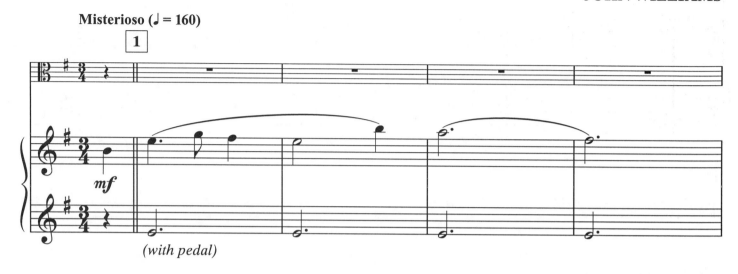

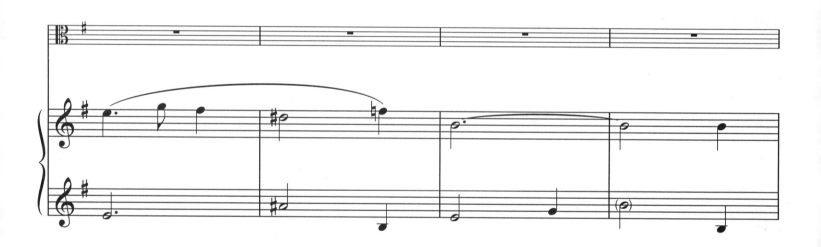

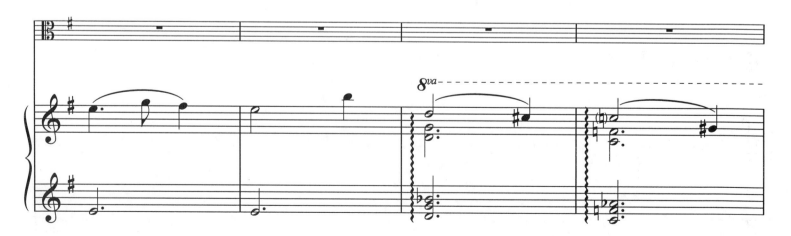

Hedwig's Theme - 5 - 1
IFM0427CD

© 2001 WARNER-BARHAM MUSIC, LLC (BMI)
All Rights Administered by WARNER-TAMERLANE PUBLISHING CORP. (BMI)
All Rights Reserved

* A# = Bb.

51 Bright (♩ = 80)

The Very Best of
John Williams
INSTRUMENTAL SOLOS

CD INCLUDED

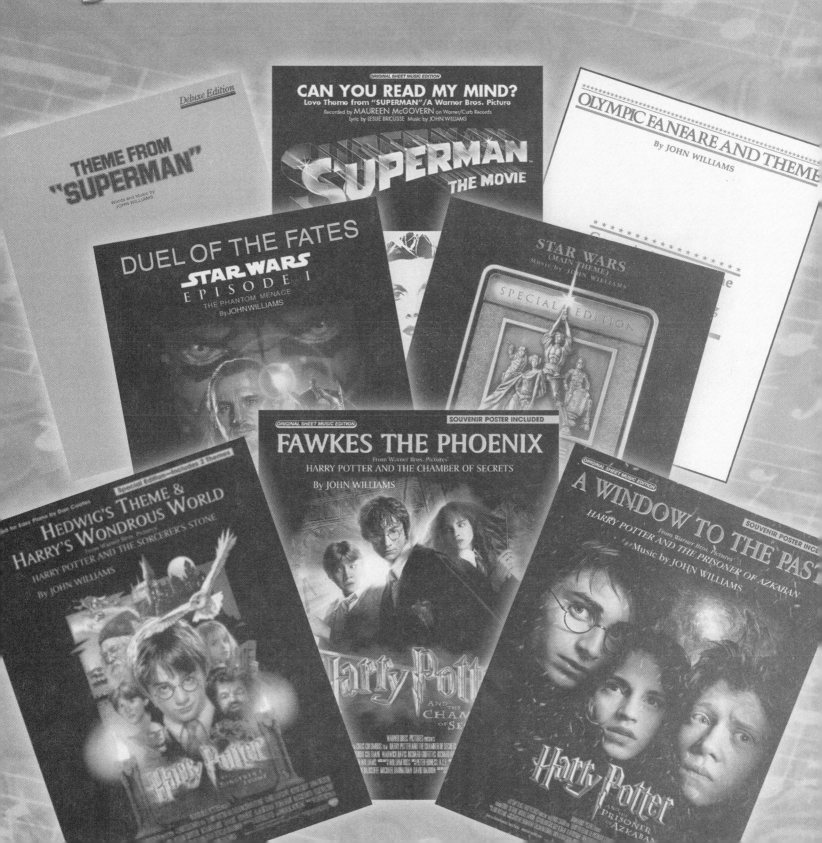

John Williams

John Williams was born in New York and moved to Los Angeles with his family in 1948. There he attended UCLA, Los Angeles City College, and studied composition privately with Mario Castelnuovo-Tedesco. After service in the Air Force, Mr. Williams returned to New York to attend Juilliard University, where he studied piano with Madame Rosina Lhevinne. While in New York, he also worked as a jazz pianist, both in clubs and on recordings. He then returned to Los Angeles, where he began his career in the film industry, working with such composers as Bernard Herrmann, Alfred Newman, and Franz Waxman. He went on to write music for many television programs in the 1960s, winning four Emmy Awards for his work.

Mr. Williams has composed the music and served as a music director for more than one hundred films, including *The Terminal, Harry Potter and the Prisoner of Azkaban, Harry Potter and the Chamber of Secrets, Minority Report, Star Wars*: Episode II *Attack of the Clones, Harry Potter and the Sorcerer's Stone, A.I. Artificial Intelligence, The Patriot, Angela's Ashes, Star Wars*: Episode I *The Phantom Menace, Stepmom, Saving Private Ryan, Amistad, Seven Years in Tibet, The Lost World, Rosewood, Sleepers, Nixon, Sabrina, Schindler's List, Jurassic Park, Home Alone, Home Alone 2, Far and Away, JFK, Hook, Presumed Innocent, Born on the Fourth of July*, the *Indiana Jones* trilogy, *The Accidental Tourist, Empire of the Sun, The Witches of Eastwick, E.T. (the Extra-Terrestrial), Superman, Close Encounters of the Third Kind*, the *Star Wars* trilogy, *Jaws*, and *Goodbye, Mr. Chips*. He has received forty-two Academy Award nominations, most recently for his score from Steven Spielberg's latest film *Catch Me If You Can*, making him the Academy's most nominated living person. He has been awarded five Oscars, three British Academy Awards, eighteen Grammys, three Golden Globes, four Emmys, and numerous gold and platinum records.

In January 1980, Mr. Williams was named nineteenth conductor of the Boston Pops Orchestra since its founding in 1885. He currently holds the title of Boston Pops laureate conductor, which he assumed following his retirement in December 1993 after fourteen highly successful seasons. Mr. Williams also holds the title of artist-in-residence at Tanglewood.

Mr. Williams has written many concert pieces, including two symphonies, a cello concerto premiered by Yo-Yo Ma and the Boston Symphony Orchestra at Tanglewood in 1994, concertos for the flute and violin recorded by the London Symphony Orchestra, concertos for the clarinet and tuba, and a trumpet concerto, which was premiered by the Cleveland Orchestra and their principal trumpet Michael Sachs in September 1996. His bassoon concerto, "The Five Sacred Trees," which was premiered by the New York Philharmonic and principal bassoon player Judith LeClair in 1995, was recorded by Mr. Williams with Ms. LeClair and the London Symphony Orchestra and has recently been released by Sony Classical to critical acclaim. In addition, Mr. Williams has composed the well-known NBC theme "The Mission," "Liberty Fanfare" composed for the rededication of the Statue of Liberty, "We're Lookin Good!" composed for the Special Olympics in celebration of the 1987 International Summer Games, and themes for the 1984, 1988, and 1996 Summer Olympic games and the 2002 Winter Olympic Games.

His concert work "Seven for Luck" for soprano and orchestra, a seven-piece song cycle based on the texts of former U.S. Poet Laureate Rita Dove, was given its world premiere by the Boston Symphony under Mr. Williams with soprano Cynthia Haymon at Tanglewood in 1998. Mr. Williams also composed his "American Journey," an orchestral work written to commemorate the new millennium and to accompany the retrospective film *The Unfinished Journey* directed by Steven Spielberg. The film and music were premiered at the "America's Millennium" concert in Washington, D.C., New Year's Eve 1999. Mr. Williams recently premiered a new concerto for French horn and orchestra, a work that was commissioned by the Chicago Symphony Orchestra for their principal horn, Dale Clevenger.

Many of Mr. Williams' film scores have been released as recordings; the soundtrack album *Star Wars* has sold more than four million copies, making it one of the most successful non-pop albums in recording history. Mr. Williams' highly acclaimed series of albums with the Boston Pops Orchestra began in 1980 on the Philips label, for which he recorded *Pops in Space; Pops on the March; Aisle Seat; Pops Out of This World; With a Song in My Heart* (a collaboration with soprano Jessye Norman); *America, the Dream Goes On* (a collection of favorite Americana); *Swing, Swing, Swing; Pops in Love; By Request...* (featuring music composed by John Williams); Holst's *The Planets; Salute to Hollywood*; and an all-Gershwin album entitled *Pops by George*. In 1990, John Williams and the Boston Pops started making recordings exclusively for the Sony Classical label. To date, these have included *Music of the Night* (an album of contemporary and classical show tunes); *I Love a Parade* (a collection of favorite marches); *The Spielberg/Williams Collaboration* (featuring John Williams' music for Steven Spielberg's films); *The Green Album* (which includes "This Land Is Your Land," "Simple Gifts," and "Theme for Earth Day"); a Christmas album entitled *Joy to the World*; an album of music by George Gershwin, Cole Porter, Richard Rodgers, and Jerome Kern entitled *Unforgettable*; a tribute to Frank Sinatra entitled *Night and Day*; an album featuring music by John Williams and Aaron Copland entitled *Music for Stage and Screen*; *It Don't Mean a Thing If It Ain't Got That Swing*, with vocalist Nancy Wilson; and *Williams on Williams: The Classic Spielberg Scores*. Mr. Williams' most recent recording with the Boston Pops Orchestra is entitled *Summon the Heroes*, the title track of which was the official theme for the 1996 Summer Olympics in Atlanta.

Mr. Williams has led the Boston Pops Esplanade Orchestra on United States tours in 1985, 1989, and 1992 and on a tour of Japan in 1987. He led the Boston Pops Orchestra on tours of Japan in 1990 and 1993. In addition to leading the Boston Symphony Orchestra at Symphony Hall and at Tanglewood, Mr. Williams has appeared as guest conductor with a number of major orchestras, including the London Symphony, the Cleveland Orchestra, the Philadelphia Orchestra, the Chicago Symphony, the Pittsburgh Symphony, the Dallas Symphony, the San Francisco Symphony, and the Los Angeles Philharmonic, with which he has appeared many times at the Hollywood Bowl. Mr. Williams holds honorary degrees from twenty American universities, including The Juilliard School, Berklee College of Music in Boston, Boston College, Northeastern University, Tufts University, Boston University, the New England Conservatory of Music, the University of Massachusetts at Boston, The Eastman School of Music, and the Oberlin Conservatory of Music. Mr. Williams also recently served as the grand marshal of the 2004 Rose Parade in Pasadena.

(June 2004)

Contents

CANTINA BAND

Music by
JOHN WILLIAMS

Moderately fast ragtime (♩ = 112)

To Coda ⊕

Cantina Band - 2 - 1
IFM0427CD

© 1977 WARNER-TAMERLANE PUBLISHING CORP. (BMI) and BANTHA MUSIC (BMI)
All Rights Administered by WARNER-TAMERLANE PUBLISHING CORP.
All Rights Reserved

D.S. % al Coda

⊕ *Coda*

Cantina Band - 2 - 2
IFM0427CD

DUEL OF THE FATES

Music by
JOHN WILLIAMS

Duel of the Fates - 2 - 1
IFM0427CD

© 1999 Bantha Music (BMI)
All Rights Administered by WARNER-TAMERLANE PUBLISHING CORP.
All Rights Reserved

FAWKES THE PHOENIX

Music by
JOHN WILLIAMS

© 2002 WARNER-BARHAM MUSIC, LLC (BMI)
All Rights Administered by WARNER-TAMERLANE PUBLISHING CORP. (BMI)
All Rights Reserved

*An easier 8th-note alternative figure has been provided.

HARRY'S WONDROUS WORLD

Music by
JOHN WILLIAMS

Harry's Wondrous World - 3 - 1
IFM0427CD

© 2001 WARNER-BARHAM MUSIC, LLC (BMI)
All Rights Administered by WARNER-TAMERLANE PUBLISHING CORP. (BMI)
All Rights Reserved

12

*The top cue notes are provided as a performing alternative.

Harry's Wondrous World - 3 - 3
IFM0427CD

HEDWIG'S THEME

Music by
JOHN WILLIAMS

*A♯ = B♭.

IFM0427CD

© 2001 WARNER-BARHAM MUSIC, LLC (BMI)
All Rights Administered by WARNER-TAMERLANE PUBLISHING CORP. (BMI)
All Rights Reserved

THE IMPERIAL MARCH
(Darth Vader's Theme)

Music by
JOHN WILLIAMS

IFM0427CD

© 1980 WARNER-TAMERLANE PUBLISHING CORP. (BMI) and BANTHA MUSIC (BMI)
All Rights Administered by WARNER-TAMERLANE PUBLISHING CORP.
All Rights Reserved

STAR WARS
(Main Title)

Music by
JOHN WILLIAMS

Majestically, steady march (♩ = 108)

IFM0427CD

© 1977 WARNER-TAMERLANE PUBLISHING CORP. (BMI) and BANTHA MUSIC (BMI)
All Rights Administered by WARNER-TAMERLANE PUBLISHING CORP.
All Rights Reserved

MAY THE FORCE BE WITH YOU

Music by
JOHN WILLIAMS

IFM0427CD

© 1980 WARNER-TAMERLANE PUBLISHING CORP. and BANTHA MUSIC (BMI)
All Rights Administered by WARNER-TAMERLANE PUBLISHING CORP. (BMI)
All Rights Reserved

CAN YOU READ MY MIND?
(Love Theme From "Superman")

Words by
LESLIE BRICUSSE

Music by
JOHN WILLIAMS

IFM0427CD

© 1978 WARNER-TAMERLANE PUBLISHING CORP. (BMI)
All Rights Reserved

OLYMPIC FANFARE AND THEME

(1984 Olympic Games)

Music by
JOHN WILLIAMS

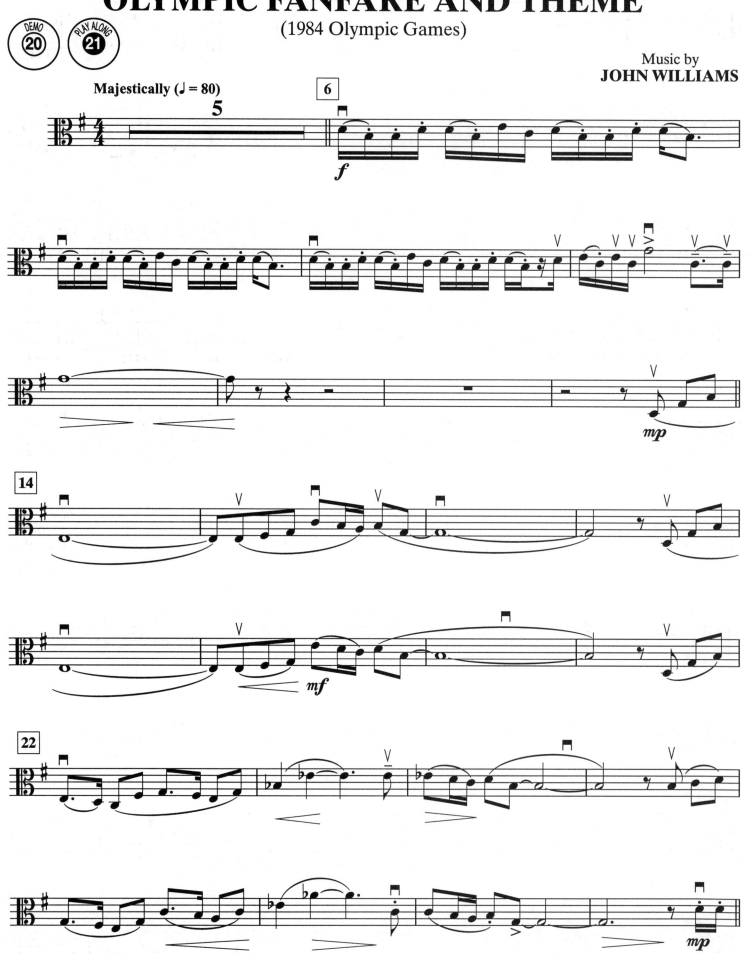

Olympic Fanfare and Theme - 2 - 1
IFM0427CD

© 1984 WARNER-TAMERLANE PUBLISHING CORP. (BMI) and MARJER PUBLISHING CO. (BMI)
All Rights Administered by WARNER-TAMERLANE PUBLISHING CORP.
All Rights Reserved

Olympic Fanfare and Theme - 2 - 2
IFM0427CD

THEME FROM "SUPERMAN"

DEMO **22** PLAY ALONG **23**

Music by
JOHN WILLIAMS

Maestoso (♩. = 76)
(Tempo click)

1

8 **March** (♩. = 112)

Theme from "Superman" - 2 - 1
IFM0427CD

© 1978 WARNER-TAMERLANE PUBLISHING CORP. (BMI)
All Rights Reserved

A WINDOW TO THE PAST

Music by
JOHN WILLIAMS

Slowly and tenderly (♩. = 54)

IFM0427CD

© 2004 Warner-Barham Music, LLC (BMI)
All Rights Administered by Warner-Tamerlane Publishing Corp. (BMI)
All Rights Reserved

DOUBLE TROUBLE

Music by
JOHN WILLIAMS

Medieval in spirit (♩ = 92)

IFM0427CD

© 2004 Warner-Barham Music, LLC (BMI)
All Rights Administered by Warner-Tamerlane Publishing Corp. (BMI)
All Rights Reserved

Unlock the Magic of Popular Music for Strings!

The Lord of the Rings Instrumental Solos for Strings

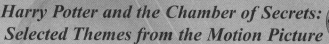

This edition offers 12 major themes from the blockbuster trilogy and includes the piano accompaniment and CD. From *The Fellowship of the Ring*: The Prophecy • In Dreams • Concerning Hobbits • Many Meetings • The Black Rider. From *The Two Towers*: Gollum's Song • Rohan • Evenstar • Forth Eorlingas. From *The Return of the King*: Into the West • The Steward of Gondor • Minas Tirith. Available for violin (IFM0412CD), viola (IFM0413CD), and cello (IFM0414CD).

Harry Potter and the Chamber of Secrets: Selected Themes from the Motion Picture

All editions are compatible and can be played separately or together. The included CD contains a demonstration of each song followed by a play-along track. *Titles are:* The Chamber of Secrets • Dobby the House Elf • Family Portrait • Fawkes the Phoenix • Gilderoy Lockhart • Harry's Wondrous World • Hedwig's Theme • Moaning Myrtle • Nimbus 2000. Available for violin (IFM0247CD), viola (IFM0248CD), and cello (IFM0249CD).

Paul Revere Award Winner

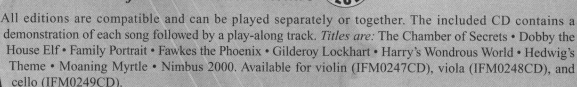

Movie Instrumental Solos for Strings

Available with an accompaniment CD, including a demo track and a play-along track. *Titles are:* In Dreams (from *The Lord of the Rings: The Fellowship of the Ring*) • Across the Stars (from *Star Wars*®: Episode II *Attack of the Clones*) • Duel of the Fates (from *Star Wars*®: Episode I *The Phantom Menace*) • Fawkes the Phoenix (from *Harry Potter and the Chamber of Secrets*) • Gollum's Song (from *The Lord of the Rings: The Two Towers*) • James Bond Theme (from *Die Another Day*) • Goldfinger (from *Goldfinger*) • Hedwig's Theme (from *Harry Potter and the Sorcerer's Stone*) • October Sky (from *October Sky*) • Theme from *Jurassic Park*. Available for violin (IFM0315CD), viola (IFM0316CD), and cello (IFM0317CD).

The James Bond Collection for Strings

All of the excitement of James Bond is now in an incredible collection for strings. *The James Bond Collection for Strings* features favorite James Bond movie themes with an accompaniment CD. *Titles include:* Diamonds Are Forever • For Your Eyes Only • From Russia with Love • Goldfinger • The James Bond Theme • Live and Let Die • Nobody Does It Better • On Her Majesty's Secret Service • Thunderball • Tomorrow Never Dies • The World Is Not Enough • You Only Live Twice. Available for violin (IFM0401CD), viola (IFM0402CD), and cello (IFM0403CD).

AD1172 9/04

THE IMPERIAL MARCH
(Darth Vader's Theme)

Music by
JOHN WILLIAMS

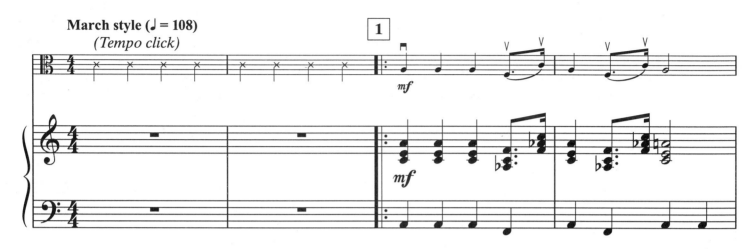

The Imperial March - 3 - 1
IFM0427CD

© 1980 WARNER-TAMERLANE PUBLISHING CORP. (BMI) and BANTHA MUSIC (BMI)
All Rights Administered by WARNER-TAMERLANE PUBLISHING CORP.
All Rights Reserved

The Imperial March - 3 - 3
IFM0427CD

STAR WARS
(Main Title)

Music by
JOHN WILLIAMS

Majestically, steady march (♩ = 108)

Star Wars - 3 - 1
IFM0427CD

© 1977 WARNER-TAMERLANE PUBLISHING CORP. (BMI) and BANTHA MUSIC (BMI)
All Rights Administered by WARNER-TAMERLANE PUBLISHING CORP.
All Rights Reserved

MAY THE FORCE BE WITH YOU

Music by
JOHN WILLIAMS

Moderately (♩ = 96)

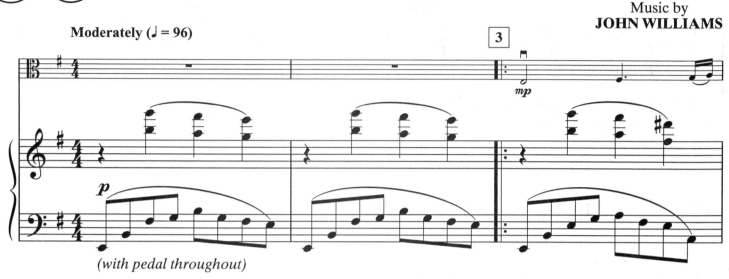

(with pedal throughout)

May the Force Be With You - 3 - 1
IFM0427CD

© 1980 WARNER-TAMERLANE PUBLISHING CORP. and BANTHA MUSIC (BMI)
All Rights Administered by WARNER-TAMERLANE PUBLISHING CORP. (BMI)
All Rights Reserved

May the Force Be With You - 3 - 3

CAN YOU READ MY MIND?

(Love Theme From "Superman")

Words by
LESLIE BRICUSSE

Music by
JOHN WILLIAMS

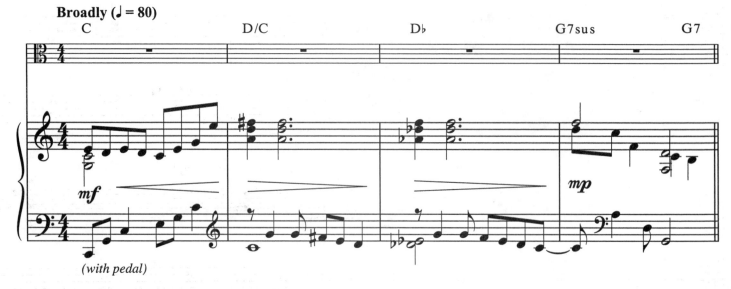

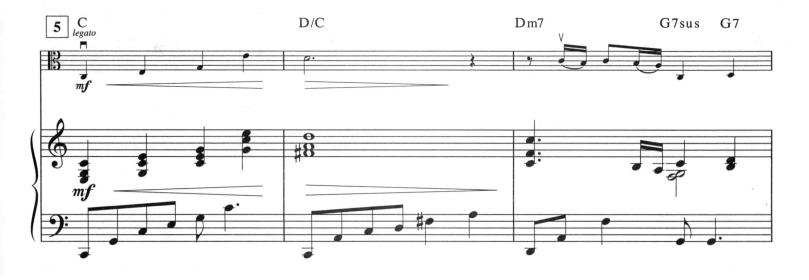

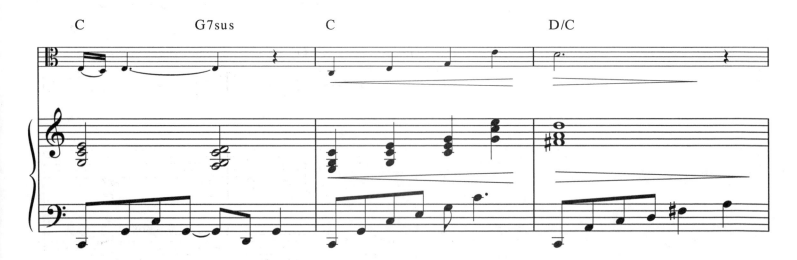

Can You Read My Mind? - 3 - 1
IFM0427CD

© 1978 WARNER-TAMERLANE PUBLISHING CORP. (BMI)
All Rights Reserved

OLYMPIC FANFARE AND THEME

(1984 Olympic Games)

Music by
JOHN WILLIAMS

Majestically (♩ = 80)

decresc. poco a poco

Olympic Fanfare and Theme - 5 - 1
IFM0427CD

© 1984 WARNER-TAMERLANE PUBLISHING CORP. (BMI) and MARJER PUBLISHING CO. (BMI)
All Rights Administered by WARNER-TAMERLANE PUBLISHING CORP.
All Rights Reserved

59

THEME FROM "SUPERMAN"

Music by
JOHN WILLIAMS

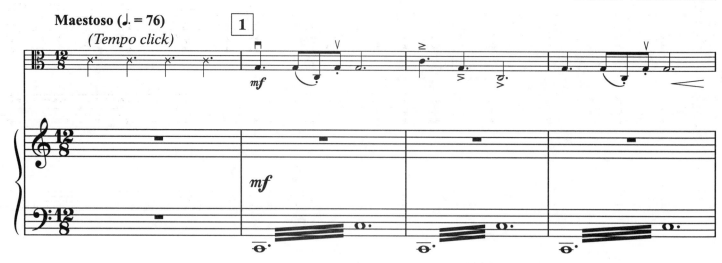

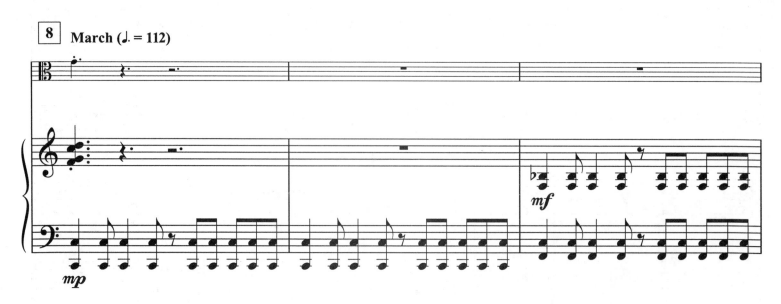

Theme from "Superman" - 6 - 1
IFM0427CD

© 1978 WARNER-TAMERLANE PUBLISHING CORP. (BMI)
All Rights Reserved

52

Theme from "Superman" - 6 - 3
IFM0427CD

A WINDOW TO THE PAST

Music by
JOHN WILLIAMS

Slowly and tenderly (♩. = 54)

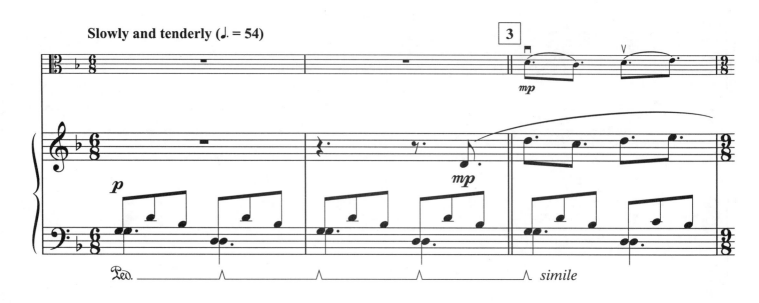

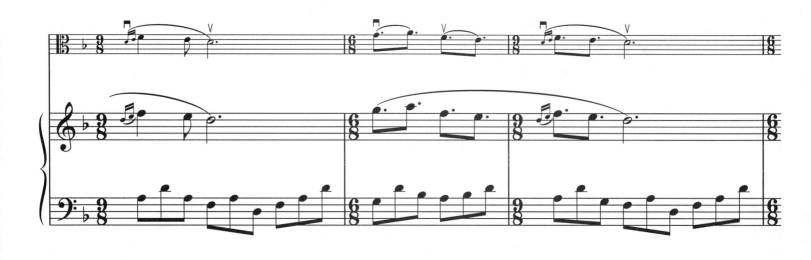

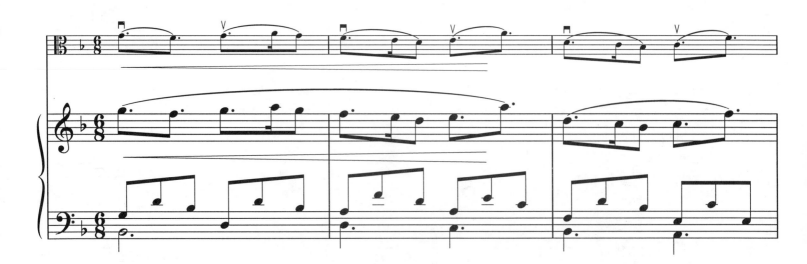

A Window to the Past - 4 - 1
IFM0427CD

© 2004 Warner-Barham Music, LLC (BMI)
All Rights Administered by Warner-Tamerlane Publishing Corp. (BMI)
All Rights Reserved